Comma Rules

When used correctly, the comma rules.

Alisa Miller

Table of Contents

Introduction

Several years ago, feeling frustrated by the rampant comma misuse I saw seemingly everywhere, I decided to start a Twitter feed focusing on correct comma usage. I didn't want to be an awful grammar dictator. I just wanted to share the correct usage in an informative, and sometimes fun, way. My Twitter feed @commarules became more popular than I expected. I believe people resonated with my positive approach to education coupled with specific examples. Over the years, I found it difficult to maintain the Twitter feed because there are a finite number of comma rules to share. When I began repeating them, I felt redundant. Every now and then, a follower would ask me if I would consider writing a book based on the Twitter account. Recently, I realized I did want to write that book. What you now have is my effort to share how to use a comma correctly in an informative, and sometimes fun, way based on @commarules. I hope this small book can become a helpful resource for those who need to write—whether you be a student, teacher, writer, or just a fan of the comma.

Thank you to those of you who have bought this book, and thank you to all the Twitter followers who inspired this book. You all have my deepest gratitude.

Alisa Miller
October 2017

Commas with Introductory Phrases

Use a comma after an introductory word, phrase, or clause.

> Well, I guess we should go home.
> When the dog barked, the baby woke up.

Use a comma after a prepositional phrase at the beginning of a sentence.

> With a camera in hand, she set out to document the world.
> After the rain, the air smelled sweet.

Introductory transitional phrases such as "in fact," "in summary," and "for example" should be followed by a comma.

> In fact, I don't like cake.
> Judy is a fan of silly humor. In particular, she enjoys puns.
> In the meantime, please hold on to your luggage.

When a dependent clause starts a sentence, it should be followed by a comma.

> While Tony enjoyed the conversation, he needed to leave before Carmela arrived.

When an adverbial dependent clause starts a sentence, a comma can provide clarity and avoid confusion.

> Unclear: When you stand up to leave your friends will say goodbye.
> Better: When you stand up to leave, your friends will say goodbye.

Commas and Conjunctions

Use this mnemonic to remember to use a comma when any of these coordinating conjunctions join two independent clauses: FANBOYS. FANBOYS indicates these coordinating conjunctions: for, and, nor, but, or, yet, and so.

Two complete sentences joined by a conjunction should have a comma.

> Tom went to the store, but he did not find what he needed to buy.

A complete sentence joined with a conjunction to a dependent phrase (an incomplete sentence) does not need a comma.

> Tom went to the store but did not find what he needed to buy.

Two complete sentences that don't have a conjunction shouldn't have a comma. This is a comma splice. Use a period or semicolon instead.

> Tom went to the store. He did not find what he needed to buy.
> Tom went to the store; he did not find what he needed to buy.

An appositive with the conjunction "or" should be set off by commas.

> The Northern Cardinal, or *Cardinalis cardinalis*, is sometimes considered a sign of good luck.

Don't use a comma before the 2nd half of a correlative conjunction (either/or, neither/nor, etc.) unless both sides have independent clauses (complete sentences).

> She wants either cake or ice cream.
> (not complete sentences.)
> Either she wants to eat cake, or she wants to eat ice cream.
> (complete sentences.)

Commas with Phrases and Clauses

Set off a contrasting phrase or clause with commas.

> Sleet, not rain, began falling in the evening.

Use commas to set off interjections and adverbial phrases that make a break in the continuity of the sentence.

> That, after all, was the best way to handle the situation.

No comma is needed after a gerund phrase acting as the subject of a sentence.

> Playing in the soccer game made Lucas happy.
> Jumping into the pool feels good on a summer day.

When a sentence ends with a participial phrase, it should be set off by a comma unless the phrase delivers vital information.

> The couple sat under the waterfall, enjoying the natural beauty.

An absolute phrase should be set off by a comma or commas, no matter its placement in the sentence.

> Their shining bodies flashing in the sun, the fish moved in unison.
> The fish, their shining bodies flashing in the sun, moved in unison.

Offset an adverbial phrase that makes a break in the sentence with commas.

> Quincy decided, in June, to buy a Christmas tree.

Do not use commas between nouns and clauses beginning with "that."

> The rain that was beginning to fall came as a relief.

Do not use a comma with a restrictive "that" clause, but do use a comma with a non-restrictive "which" clause. Restrictive "that" offers vital information to the meaning of the sentence. Non-restrictive "which" simply adds additional detail.

> Beatrice likes flowers that are red. (restrictive)
> ("That are red" provides detail about the specific flowers.)
> Beatrice likes flowers, which is sweet. (non-restrictive)
> ("Which is sweet" adds information about the situation, not the flowers.)

The two clauses in an "If...then" sentence should be separated by a comma, even when the "then" is implied.

> If it is snowing, then school will be cancelled.
> If it is snowing, school will be cancelled.

A run-on sentence (two complete sentences not separated by punctuation) can be fixed by separating the independent clauses with a semicolon, a comma and a conjunction, or a period.

> Error: My dog rules she is spunky.
> Better: My dog rules; she is spunky. (semicolon)
> Or: My dog rules, and she is spunky. (comma and a conjunction)
> Or: My dog rules. She is spunky. (period)

Short contrasting clauses can be separated by a comma without a conjunction.

> I laughed, she did not.

Use a comma with a concessive clause that begins with "even though," "although," or "though," unless it is essential to the meaning of the sentence.

> Katniss wore boots to the arena, although I prefer sandals.
> Katniss wore boots to the arena even though it was warm outside.

If an adverb separates a compound sentence, it is preceded by a semicolon and usually followed by a comma.

> Jeeves was asked to make the guest comfortable; accordingly, he showed the queen to her room.

Comma Advice:

If a sentence has several commas, it may be clearer to the reader if it is rewritten.

Commas and Specific Words

Using a comma with the word "too" is optional. Use the comma to provide emphasis.

> He made effective changes too.
> He made effective changes, too.
> He, too, made effective changes.

Commas should always set off "yes," "no, " and all casual forms of these two words in sentences.

> Yes, I heard what you said.
> Why, no, I do not wear socks on my head.
> Yeah, I'm going to the party tonight.
> Nope, I don't want to do my homework.

While it is not required, it is recommended that "et cetera" and "etc." be set off by commas.

> Andraya brought cake, balloons, candles, etc., to the birthday celebration.

A comma usually precedes and almost always follows "i.e." and "e.g."

> Michael loves eating spicy foods, e.g., Thai and Mexican.
> Spicy food is often found in Latin American countries, i.e., most of Central and South America.

Use a comma or an exclamation point after an interjection.

> Ouch, that really hurt.
> Hey! That's my toe.

Use a comma between two adjectives that both modify the same noun.
If you can use "and" between the adjectives or reverse the adjectives,
then use a comma.

>The child's blonde, curly hair is beautiful.
>The old stone fence runs along the meadow.

Don't use a comma in a compound predicate (two or more verbs that
share the same subject).

>Error: I spoke to the manager, and relayed my concerns.
>Correct: I spoke to the manager and relayed my concerns.

Starting a sentence with "however" requires a comma if you mean
"nevertheless."

>However, Ethan attempted to run the race despite a swollen knee.

"However" at the beginning of a sentence is not followed by a comma
if you mean "in whatever manner."

>However you want to arrange the furniture in the room is fine with
>me.

When using "however" in the middle of a sentence, set off with
commas if it is used as an interjection.

>Adam was happy, however, that the team let him serve as the water
>boy.

When using "however" to join two complete sentences, set it off with a
semicolon and a comma.

>The new shoes hurt Katy's feet; however, she had no other shoes to
>wear.

Commas for Clarity

Separate consecutive uses of the same word with a comma if it will help make the meaning clearer.

> What is, is.
> The bride walked in, in her wedding dress.

Do not insert a single comma between the subject and predicate unless it will prevent misunderstanding.

> Error: The special collection at the museum, is on display through the month.
> Correct: The special collection at the museum is on display through the month.

Commas are sometimes necessary to prevent readers misunderstanding the meaning of the sentence.

> Confusing: For Kate Miles was a hero.
> Clear: For Kate, Miles was a hero.
> Confusing: When you remember to call your parents are happy.
> Clear: When you remember to call, your parents are happy.

When a word or phrase adds more detail to the noun, it is offset by commas.

> Elsie's sister, a dairy farmer, could answer our questions about raw milk.

Serial Commas

To reduce confusion when creating a series of words or ideas, include the comma after each item, including the final one before the "and." This is known as a serial comma.

    Confusing: We had chicken, salad, macaroni and cheese for dinner.
    Clear: We had chicken, salad, macaroni, and cheese for dinner.

A compound sentence consisting of short independent clauses and a conjunction should contain commas in the same manner as a series.

    She saw him, she screamed, and he dropped the TV on his foot.

Few punctuation marks enjoy such controversy as the serial comma, also known as an Oxford comma or a Harvard comma. While most style guides recommend using the serial comma, some people feel passionately about not using it. I prefer the clarity the serial comma provides. Even some style guides that advise omitting the serial comma in a simple series recommend using it in a complex series. In times of ambiguity, it's always best to use the comma.

Comma Advice:

Refrain from inserting commas merely to break up long sentences or to indicate where a speaker should take a breath.

Commas and Parentheses and Parenthetical Elements

If a comma is needed just following parentheses or brackets, the comma goes outside the parentheses or brackets.

> Although they rescued the boy (who was on the top floor), the firefighters still had work to do.

Parenthetical elements, information that adds detail but doesn't contribute to the meaning of the sentence, should be set off with commas. (See what I did there?)

> Emmet, the tall boy, went to the principal's office.

Parenthetical elements that are closely related to the meaning of the sentence should be set off by commas. Parenthetical elements that are less closely related to the meaning of the sentence are set off by dashes or parentheses.

> Jane, after looking for months, will be starting a new job in Paris.
> Jane—who lives in the yellow house—will be starting a new job in Paris.
> Jane (who lives in the yellow house) will be starting a new job in Paris.

Commas and Quotations

If a comma is necessary immediately following quotation marks, place the comma inside the quotation marks.

She said, "Make yourself at home," but she didn't let me in the door.

Use a comma to set off a direct quote, but not for indirect quotes. The word "that" is a good indicator it may be indirect.

Mirasole said, "I am hungry."
Mirasole said that she is hungry.

While Americans put the comma inside a closing quotation mark, the British put it inside only if it is a part of the quote.

Mr. Darcy announced, "I want to go," and he left. (American)
Mr. Darcy announced, "I want to go", and he left. (British)

Do not use a comma after "entitled" or "called" and before the quotation marks around the title.

Miss O'Connor wrote a short story called "The River."

When a quotation is not part of dialog, it is not set off by a comma.

Sally was thinking about the words in "First Love" and collided with Linus as he approached her.

Don't use commas with a quotation acting as a structural element of a sentence.

The book ends with "and the tree was happy."

Commas and Correspondence

In informal correspondence, salutations should be followed by a comma. Use a colon in formal correspondence.

> Dear Mom, I'm working again.
> Hey, how are you?
> Dear President Lincoln: I'm writing in response to your Gettysburg Address.

Always use commas with closings in correspondence, whether they are formal or informal.

> Love, Mom
> Best Regards, Lucy van Pelt

Commas and Questions

When a direct question comes before the rest of the sentence, the comma that would offset the question should be replaced by a question mark.

> Who ate that cake? Pauline wondered.

When a direct question follows an element that introduces it, the two are separated by a comma.

> Pauline wondered, where is the missing cake?

An indirect question is not offset by a comma.

> Pauline wondered about the mystery of the missing cake.

Commas with People, Titles, and Places

Use commas to set off a direct address to a person or a group of people.

> Sir, you are stepping on my foot.
> The food, my friends, is now on the table.

Use commas to set off names.

> Come here, Mark, and give me a kiss.

If a man includes a comma before the "Jr." or "Sr." in his name, a comma must follow the abbreviation as well.

> Marvin K. Mooney, Jr., wrote that book.
> Marvin K. Mooney Jr. wrote that book.

When a job title follows a person's name, the title should be set off with commas.

> Agatha Christie, Lead Editor, was the keynote speaker.

If a job title comes before a person's name and includes "a" or "an," then the name should be set off with commas.

> A creative director, Don Draper, was promoted to Junior Partner.

If a job title comes before a name and includes "the," offset with commas if only one person has that position. Do not offset if more than one person holds that position.

> The manager, Frank Hamer, called the police.
> (only one manager)
> The teller Bonnie Parker identified the bank robber.
> (more than one teller)

Commas should set off abbreviations for degrees and titles in people's names.

> Ranjana Chaudhury, Ph.D., gave a speech on the importance of energy conservation.
> Alex Holmes, M.D., taught a biology class at the local community college.

When writing place names, commas come after both the city and the state, province, or country.

> Austin, Texas, is known for its live music scene.
> We visited Munich, Germany, last summer.

Commas can be used to set off a place of residence when following a person's name.

> Fred Flintstone, of Bedrock, was present at the stonecutters' bowling tournament.

Commas on the Internet:

This animated comma can explain so much in Comma Story from TEDEd.
https://ed.ted.com/lessons/comma-story-terisa-folaron

Commas with Dates and Numbers

Commas should always follow the day and the year when writing a month-day-year series.

> Error: The party will be on December 31, 2009 at Ben's house.
> Correct: The party will be on December 31, 2009, at Ben's house.

When writing a year, a comma is not used unless the year is longer than four digits.

> 2010
> 13,245 B.C.

When describing a person's height in feet and inches, no comma is necessary.

> The student is a remarkable six feet nine inches.

Commas in Special Circumstances

Be careful of inverted sentences that might look as if they require a comma. They probably don't.

> Error: Speaking to the class, was a famous poet.
> Correct: Speaking to the class was a famous poet

Use a comma in place of omitted information that is inferred in sentences with parallel construction.

> Violet likes alternative music; Ben, heavy metal. (The word "likes" following "Ben" is inferred.)
> Her day was filled with joy; his, with sorrow.

Set off contrasting ideas with commas.

> She voted for, not against, the young candidate.

It's okay to split a compound predicate with a comma if the split stresses the passage of time.

> Hamlet was born the prince of Denmark, and killed his uncle. (He didn't kill his uncle right after he was born.)

Commas are not necessary in vertical lists (such as bulleted or numbered lists).

> Grocery list
> - Apples
> - Bread
> - Paper towels

If the items in a vertical list are phrases that complete a sentence, commas can be used after each item, and a period follows the last item.

I would like to have
- a new phone,
- new shoes,
- and a million dollars.

Comma Advice:

Commas are used to mark specific elements within a sentence to help reader understanding. Keep in mind their job is to eliminate confusion.

Friday Facts

A regular feature on my Twitter feed was the inclusion of fun facts about the comma, which I presented on Fridays. Here are some of my favorites.

The comma is the most used punctuation mark.

James Joyce sometimes agonized for days over where to place a comma.

Commas are not a representation of a breath taken during speech. They are used to identify and separate elements of a sentence.

From the 13th through the 17th centuries, the comma was actually a forward slash known as a virgula suspensiva.

In 1992, a patent was filed to invent the question comma and the exclamation comma.

Gertrude Stein was not a fan of commas, saying the use of them was "positively degrading."

In 15th century Italian manuscripts, colons were sometimes used in the manner that commas are used today.

Elocutionists of the 1700s used the colon, semicolon, and comma to indicate how long a pause to take in an oral recitation.

6 of the 20 most common errors in college essays involve comma usage, including the #1 most common error, which is not including a comma after an introductory element.

Rules of comma usage vary from language to language, even among different varieties of English.

Comma placement in a contract was at the heart of a legal debate that cost a Canadian company $2.13 million.

The Chinese language employs two different commas, including a backward-slanting comma used for separating a list of items.

The placement of a comma in the Second Amendment has sparked gun-rights controversy in the past.

Artist Jim Sanborn created a giant comma that is in front of the MD Anderson Library at University of Houston.

Grammarian EB White was known to condemn comma splices. However, Merriam-Webster documents his use of one in a letter.

Acknowledgments

Many thanks to the Twitter readers who inspired this book. Without you, this project truly would not have come alive. Thanks to Jessica, Frankie, Jennifer, Suvi, Andrea, and Coral for offering to add your input on the content. Special, loving thanks to my husband, Mark, who encouraged me to bring this project to life.